CW01023074

MURDERS IN HOLLYWOOD: TRUE CRIME STORIES OF HOMICIDE IN THE HILLS

First edition. October 20, 2021.

Copyright © 2021 Eliza Toska.

ISBN: 979-8201274283

Written by Eliza Toska.

Table of Contents

Murders in Hollywood: True Crime Stories of Homicide in the Hills

By Eliza Toska

Introduction

True crime has always fascinated me. One of the things about true crime that

intrigues me is that we are all susceptible to being victims at the hands of others. I believe that this is why the topic is so popular - we immerse ourselves in stories of true life horror so we can better understand the evil others are capable of and use the terrifying events we learn about as cautionary tales. Still - most of us believe it'll never happen to us.

When a crime occurs in affluent areas or to people who live apparently privileged lives, we seem to find these crimes almost unbelievable - things like murder and rape don't happen to these types of people. Although this archaic way of thinking is slowly eroding, it's still something I'm fascinated with. Crime in the most "unlikely" of places truly intrigues me.

When you think of luxury, hedonism, excess and a privileged way of living, perhaps - like me - you think of Hollywood. Beverley Hills and murder don't seem to naturally fit together when you picture the two in your head. Skid Row and murder will have you conjuring up images of cold-blooded killings and homeless people slaughtering each other over drugs, but to imagine brutal murders in the Hollywood hills is almost impossible. After reading this book, I'm sure it won't be.

I have, for as long as I can remember, had a love for Hollywood. I adore the notion of it, the facade perhaps, the movies it spawns and the rich history of cinema it offers. To couple this with the genre I write in felt like a fun project to embark on, so that's just what I did. In this book, I cover nine cases of people who have fallen foul to the evil that lurks in Tinseltown, the greed that turns some people deadly and the lust for blood that turns the Hollywood hills red.

The Pin-Up

Vivacious teenager Dorothy Stratten earned a living serving ice cream at her local Dairy Queen in Vancouver, Canada. While whipping up soft serves, the pretty teen caught the attention of Paul Snider, who was a local pimp always on the lookout for new women to procure. He had dreams beyond his brothel-keeping day job - he lusted after the bright lights of Hollywood.

Dorothy began working at a young age to help out her mother, who had a low-paying job in a school. The hardworking youngster had worked at Dairy Queen for four years throughout all of high school to help her mother make ends meet. Paul Snider walked in one day and spotted her immediately, changing the course of Dorothy's life forever. It was 1978, and as soon as Snider clapped eyes on Dorothy, he saw an abundance of opportunity. The 18-year-old was striking, but she was unaware of her attractiveness. She was peppy and friendly and had a trusting nature, traits which manipulative Snider knew would help him groom her.

Snider was already making a pretty steady living as a promoter for car and cycling shows. However, it wasn't enough to fund his extravagant tastes or penchant for lavish purchases. To fill in this financial deficit, he began to acquire young girls and pimp them out as a sort of side-hustle. Still, he made sure he looked the part. He drove a black, private plate Corvette, and his go-to outfit was a mink coat with encrusted jewellery hanging from his neck.

Snider had cemented himself as a predator, an opportunist, and as someone looking for his golden ticket to get him where he wanted to be. However, for a young Dorothy, whose youth and naivety were attributes to be preyed upon by Snider, the older man was complimentary and kind. In reality, he was using Dorothy's insecurities against her.

He would heap compliments on the things she felt most vulnerable about, and he'd make sure he adorned her with expensive presents and took her out to nice restaurants. He bought the gown she wore to her senior prom, and Dorothy took the older man as her date. He was 26. The manipulative man had wormed his way into every aspect of the teen's life, unfazed by how his accompanying her to prom looked to all her teenage peers.

Hollywood Calls... And Paul Snider Answers

Playboy hosted the *Great Playmate Hunt* in 1978, a contest intended to scout a brand new Playmate to star in the coveted centrefold of its 25th-anniversary issue. This competition was on Snider's radar, and he got to work convincing his 18-year-old girlfriend to be photographed in the nude for the contest. She was hesitant, to say the least - she said no initially - but Snider chipped away at her for weeks. He knew how to get to her, too. Dorothy and her mother had been living paycheck to paycheck, but Snider was feeding her ideas that life didn't have to be like this; fortune and a better future awaited her if she did as he asked. She caved and braved the professional photoshoot where she had to bare all.

MURDERS IN HOLLYWOOD: TRUE CRIME STORIES OF HOMICIDE IN THE HILLS

The photographer immediately sent the nude pictures to Playboy. When the magazine saw the test shots, a flight to Los Angeles was booked for Dorothy by the company. Snider accompanied her during her first time on an aeroplane and inside of a limo. It was noted that Dorothy was like a fish out of water here, not used to the luxurious surroundings, and unlike other Playboy models, she was unaware of her beauty. She was an anomaly, but she was a hit with the team at the Playboy office. While here, she did some test shots for them before they sent her on her way home, telling her they'd be in touch if she made the cut.

Mario Casilli was the photographer who took these shots, and he recalled that she was statuesque in looks but very child-like when spoken to. Perhaps, then, it was her shyness or her lack of confidence that saw Playboy give the centrefold to someone else. Candy Loving, a senior attending the University of Oklahoma, won the competition.

Dorothy's shyness meant she needed a lot of prompting, a lot of grooming from Snider, and special attention paid to her lack of confidence. While she didn't win the centrefold competition, she still impressed Hugh Hefner, and he crowned her Miss August 1979. He also gave her work as a Playboy Bunny at the Playboy Club in Century City, Los Angeles. Due to her young age, she wasn't allowed to serve alcohol, but she did a fine job of welcoming guests, greeting them as they made their way into the club. The new crowd she found herself rubbing shoulders with took a shine to her.

In what felt like the blink of an eye, Dorothy found herself thrust into some of Hollywood's most exclusive parties and get-togethers. Although she was excited, it was brand new to her; she was also overwhelmed by it all, and when she felt out of place or needed some advice, she turned to the one person who always knew the right thing to do: Paul Snider. Even mid-photoshoot, she would be on the phone to Snider, telling him how it was going, listening to his advice and leaning on him for the emotional support she so needed in this unfamiliar territory. Dorothy thought her newfound success was all down to her partner, and she believed she owed him a great deal for pushing her into the success she was enjoying.

The Beginning of The End For Dorothy and Snider

Playboy welcomed Dorothy into its world with open arms, and her time as a firm favourite within the company didn't seem to be waning. The more Dorothy was mingling with celebrities, doing photoshoots and partying with her fellow Playboy stars, the more Snider found himself on the outskirts of her life. It's not that Dorothy did this on purpose; it was her job. It didn't help that Paul Snider didn't make a great impression on those who were a part of Dorothy's new circle. His offensive attitude and his effort to "look the part" didn't endear him to those at the Playboy Mansion. An acquaintance of Snider later told The Canadian Press that most people who met him didn't like him and that his brash, demanding persona was off-putting.

On one occasion, Snider was drinking in the mansion's water-filled grotto, trying his luck with the girls who were in that area. He managed to catch the attention of a young girl, but he wasn't discreet about lavishing her with affection; Dorothy's make-up artist caught the pair, and Snider was kicked out of the mansion by security. He was barred from coming back unless, of course, he came with Dorothy, and she was okay with him being on the property.

In early 1979, Snider had moved to LA full-time, meaning he went wherever Dorothy went. Despite his infidelities, his hold over his younger girlfriend was as strong as ever, and in June that year, the couple married. Hugh Hefner, among other people who knew Dorothy, opposed the marriage. Perhaps the rising starlet went through with the marriage because she felt indebted to Snider. It was well-known that Dorothy felt like this new life of luxury she was living was because of him, and since he'd moved to LA, he relied upon her to support him.

By this point, Hefner had ensured Stratten had a manager to help her take care of her money as well as someone to oversee all of her work commitments. This left Paul Snider on the outskirts; he no longer had an overall say in what work Dorothy accepted or what she should do with her newfound abundance of cash. With a small team of professionals guiding the young woman into the spotlight, it wasn't long before Dorothy found herself on TV. In 1979, she starred in Playboy's *Roller Disco and Pajama Party*, which led to even bigger gigs - real acting jobs. She was landing small roles here and there, including the TV drama *Fantasy Island*. Then, in 1980, her star power was turned up a notch when she was named Playboy's Playmate of the Year as well as bagging the title role in *Galaxina*, a fantasy-comedy movie that's now got a cult following.

Dorothy was working a lot. From her Playboy commitments to her foray into acting, she was jumping out of her comfort zone and learning how to navigate Hollywood, which meant she wasn't home as much with Snider. Despite this, those around her noticed she was happy - the happiest they'd seen her. Work had afforded the young woman some time away from her controlling spouse, and the freedom and lack of suppression this gave her was clear to see.

She was drifting away from Snider, but he saw her as property - she was his. She belonged to *him*. He made her who she was - it was down to him that she'd ever stepped foot in Hollywood. Despite his warped views - and his ability to make Dorothy believe them as truth - there was no denying his grip over his younger girlfriend was weakening.

The rising star met filmmaker Peter Bogdanovich around this time. He was fresh out of a long-term relationship and began spending his free time socialising at the Playboy Mansion, in between various movie-making projects. He was instantly smitten with Dorothy, even going as far as writing her a part in his new film, *They All Laughed*, which boasted an all-star cast, including Audrey Hepburn. If there was ever the opportunity to go from pin-up to serious movie star, this was it, and Dorothy grabbed it by both hands.

While Peter was undeniably attracted to Dorothy, he didn't let her know this straight away. It was mid-production of the movie when he eventually let her know his true feelings - that he was deeply in love with her.

Dorothy Begins to Wriggle From Snider's Grip

As Snider's control over Dorothy and her career were forcibly loosened by her finding her feet in Hollywood, he became desperate. He knew she was not only becoming more successful but also more confident; this newfound self-awareness meant that Snider's manipulation didn't have the effect it once did on Dorothy. In a state of exasperation, he tried to persuade her to start a project with him, one they'd planned to do before they got married. However, when Dorothy was presented with the poster design for the production, she declined to proceed with it. Whatever grip Snider once had over Dorothy was now well and truly gone. As well as losing his power, he also lost his only source of income.

At this point, Snider had to confront the realisation that he wasn't as much of a big shot as he thought he was. With Dorothy removing herself from his life, he found that the flock of admirers was gone - they weren't ever there for him, it was always for Dorothy. He didn't own anything. He had no skills or any contacts in Hollywood that would even return his calls, including Hugh Hefner. Snider was sinking in his lack of control over his new life in LA. It hadn't turned out as he planned it to. He was spiralling into the depths of frustration and desperation.

During this descent, he met teenager Patti Laurman, a grocery store clerk whom he tried to use to emulate Dorothy's success. He wanted to turn her into the next big Playboy model, and the young woman moved into the West Los Angeles apartment Snider had shared with Dorothy and their housemate, Stephen Cushner. Still, he didn't disguise his heartbreak of losing

Dorothy in front of her. He'd cry, he'd get upset about how she no longer told him she loved him, and he even got his guitar out to play songs he wrote for his lost love. But, there was nothing Snider could do - Dorothy had finally seen through his controlling ways and was now dating Peter Bogdanovich. She moved in with him once they'd wrapped filming *They All Laughed*. Still, kind-hearted Dorothy wanted an amicable split and wanted to ensure Snider didn't struggle financially with her leaving. She wanted to arrange a settlement that would allow him to continue living in LA.

Snider, however, had other ideas. While Dorothy was considering her ex's needs after their split, he was trying to procure a gun. A friend lent him a .38 revolver, which Snider took with him to Bogdanovich's house and waited outside. The voyeuristic event saw the gun remain unused, and Snider returned the firearm to his friend. Still, his violent urges remained. He wanted to hurt those who'd hurt him, who'd stolen his Hollywood dream away.

Snider purchased his own 12-gauge shotgun on August 13, 1980.

The following day, Dorothy headed over to the place she once shared with Snider in an attempt to negotiate the settlement with him for their divorce. Those around her were dubious about Dorothy going to visit Snider alone; he wasn't to be trusted, and her new crowd of friends didn't exactly like him. Even before the split, she lied to friends, coworkers, even Hugh Hefner about seeing Snider. She had to sneak dates with him and lie about where she'd been. But now, she was being honest because she was finally free of the man who'd once been her puppet master. She arranged the meet, and Snider made sure the apartment was empty for her arrival.

Stephen Cushner and Patti Laurman arrived back home later that day. They noticed Dorothy's car outside, her Mercury Cougar parked near Snider's Mercedes, which had the private plate "STAR 80". The vanity plate would later provide the name of the title for Dorothy's biopic.

Snider's two roommates were sitting watching TV upstairs under the assumption that he and Dorothy had made up and decided to leave the pair downstairs in privacy. Still, they'd been in Snider's room for hours without a peep - it was unusual for the former couple. After hours of silence, the concerned roommates agreed to knock on Snider's bedroom door to see if everything was okay, but there was no reply. Unconvinced they were just sleeping, Stephen opened the door. What he and Patti witnessed would horrify them for the rest of their lives.

Snider and Dorothy were laid naked in the bedroom. Dorothy had been shot in the face. Both of them were dead. Patti couldn't believe it was real - it looked like a scene from a horror movie, the pools of blood and dead bodies didn't look lifelike.

Snider had lured Dorothy to his place under the guise of sorting out their split amicably. Perhaps he wanted to try and win her back, to talk her into doing what he wanted like she always had. Maybe he had always intended to rape her then shoot her in the face before turning the 12-gauge on himself. Relentlessly harbouring the need for power, rape would be the ultimate clawback of control for narcissistic Snider. By then brutally murdering her, he retained control over anybody ever else being able to have Dorothy. If Snider had no future with her, then he'd make sure nobody else would. By then shooting himself in the head, he'd never have to face the repercussions or fallout of his depraved actions.

Police estimated that Snider shot himself an hour after he killed Dorothy, so it could be he was either mustering up the courage to pull the trigger, or he was spending that time trying to work out an exit plan. In the hallway was Dorothy's handbag, still holding the thousands of dollars she had in it to give to Snider. It seems she didn't even have the opportunity to discuss their split before he turned aggressive.

When the story broke, it sent an explosion of shock through Hollywood. Those who'd crossed paths with arrogant Snider knew he was sticking his middle finger up to everyone. To the Hollywood that had rejected him, to the people who'd warned Dorothy of him, and to Dorothy herself for leaving him.

Bogdonavich was utterly devastated by the loss, as was Hugh Hefner. Bogdonavich chose the wording on her tombstone, an Ernest Hemingway quote. It starts, "If people bring so much courage to this world, the world has to kill them to break them."

Her new partner went on to take care of her family after she was murdered, including Dorothy's little sister, Louise. He kindly reasoned that if he'd had the opportunity to go through with marrying Dorothy, her family would've been his family, so he would treat them as such. Eventually, his relationship with

Dorothy's sister developed into something more than friendship, and the pair got married eight years after Dorothy was killed. Despite their 2001 divorce, the two remain close.

Dorothy Stratten was just a young, promising 20 year old when she met her unimaginably horrific end. She was on the road to becoming a star, and her career was tipped to have followed the same vein as Julia Roberts'. Her trusting nature and naïveté to the world she'd stepped into saw Paul Snider use those things against her to snuff her out so callously. His jealousy, desire for control and inability to accept rejection resulted in a young woman's life ending in the most horrifying way. The fear she must've felt in her final moments, compounded by the betrayal and heartbreak she experienced in the knowledge it was someone she trusted doing this to her, is an overwhelming thought.

The Obsessive Fan Turned Murderer

Twenty-one-year-old Rebecca Schaeffer was in the midst of preparing for the biggest audition of her career when she was shot dead by her obsessed stalker. Her murder happened before stalking was a crime, so it's hard not to imagine the budding star being alive today if her harasser had been apprehended for his unwanted and attention prior to callously shooting her.

Rebecca played a teen on the CBS show *My Sister Sam*, the premise of the show being the events that ensue when the youngster moves to San Francisco to live with her photographer sister. The sitcom was her first main role after a handful of acting jobs, and the part saw Rebecca rapidly become a firm favourite for tweens and teens, particularly those who read *Seventeen*, which she graced the cover of in March 1987.

Although *My Sister Sam* was cancelled in 1988 after just two seasons - as series' routinely are when ratings don't quite hit the numbers they're expected to - the acting jobs kept rolling in for a determined Rebecca. She co-starred in the movie *Scenes From the Class Struggle in Beverly Hills* and had finished filming a TV movie called *Voyage of Terror: The Achille Lauro Affair*. She'd also wrapped on a film directed by Dyan Cannon, called *The End of Innocence*, proving that Rebecca Schaeffer wasn't your typical Hollywood starving artist - she was most certainly going places. If there was any doubt of her superstar potential, she was also said to have been a strong contender for the lead role in forthcoming rom-com titled *Pretty Woman*.

On a typically sunny morning of July 18, 1989, the young actor was sitting inside her apartment, eagerly awaiting a delivery that could potentially change her life.

She was due to audition for the much sought-after role of Michael Corleone's daughter, Mary, in Part III of the *Godfather* trilogy. On that fateful day in July, she was scheduled to meet with Francis Ford Coppola and his crew, and the important package she was waiting for was the script for the anticipated movie. Restless and excited for the delivery, Rebecca paced her West Hollywood apartment, eager for the doorbell to ring. At 10:15 am, it did.

Rebecca answered the door, but it wasn't the postman as she'd expected, but instead 19-year-old Robert John Bardo. The teenager had been obsessed with Rebecca since he was 16 and even spent $300 on a private investigator to find out where she was living. The investigator was easily able to obtain her address from public DMV records. Bardo enlisted the help of his older brother in order to get a gun as he'd previously foiled his own attempt when he told the owner of the gun store about his mental health problems.

Before getting his little brother the gun, Edward Bardo told Robert that he must only use the gun for target practice and could only use the weapon when they were together. After agreeing to these stipulations, Edward handed over the .357 Magnum. Bardo wouldn't keep his end of the bargain.

A Teenage Crush Turns Obsessive

Bardo was still a freshman at high school when he first laid eyes on Rebecca Schaeffer in a *My Sister Sam* commercial. That summer of '86 saw the teen become obsessive about the pretty girl he saw on the screen, with his attraction to her gradually developing into something more unhealthy. He started to feel that he and Rebecca were soul mates, each of them shy and genuine, and he sought out ways to connect with his "kindred spirit." He began to send the actress tokens of his misguided and increasingly deranged affection. He penned her numerous letters, and when Rebecca replied to one of them, Robert immediately took that as a sign he ought to travel from Tucson to Los Angeles to meet her. After all, they were destined to be together.

He headed to the studio where Rebecca was working with flowers in one hand and a stuffed teddy in the other, but clearly looking like a lovesick fan, he never made it through studio security. He was insistent that he was allowed in. However, he told security he loved Rebecca Schaeffer and needed to see her, which no doubt only reinforced security's bid to ensure this young man got nowhere near the actress.

Rebecca's stylist, Judy Crown, who worked on *My Sister Sam*, noted that Schaeffer was "beautiful" and "sweet", but also "a little bit naive." Judy warned Rebecca about her obsessed fan when the flurries of letters and gifts from Bardo arrived on set. "Don't respond," the veteran stylist told her, forewarning her about the implications of engaging with people who were unhinged, which she believed this crazed fan was.

Gradually, Bardo's opinion of Rebecca shifted. He went from holding her up on a pedestal to feeling betrayed by her. His increasing anger toward her reached a peak when he watched the film *Scenes From the Class Struggle*, where she had a love scene. After becoming upset by Rebecca partaking in a romantic scene with another man, he packed his gun and bullets and boarded a bus to Los Angeles.

Rebecca was unwaveringly kind and trusting, so the idea that the author of some of the sweet letters she received could ever snap and try to harm her hadn't ever crossed her mind. She didn't think about the bad people in the world, nor did she ever think her position as an attractive actress could lead those kinds of people toward her. Her naive nature was clear to see by her behaviour when she opened the door only to be met with a stranger, not the postman she was expecting.

When she first answered the door, Rebecca was disheartened that it wasn't the script delivery she was expecting, but instead a sombre-looking Bardo. He showed her the letter she'd written him along with the autographed photo. He was her biggest fan, he told her, and Rebecca politely engaged with the fan for a short while before explaining to him that she had an interview to prepare for. "Please take care," she warmly told Bardo as she politely stepped back into the building and closed the door after shaking his hand.

Bardo was heartbroken. Unsure what to do next, he headed to a nearby diner, gathering his thoughts. After a short while simmering, he went back to Rebecca's apartment. He said he'd forgotten to give her some gifts he'd brought her: a homemade CD and yet another one of his gushing letters.

A little impatient and exasperated this time, Rebecca said to Bardo, "You came to my door again," clearly disappointed that the knock at the door wasn't her script but Bardo once again. The obsessed fan would later say that this made him feel like he was bothering her, and his emotions were yet again inadvertently injured by the Hollywood starlet. According to Bardo, that was an incredibly callous thing to say to him, and he snapped.

"I forgot to give you something," he mumbled nervously before quickly pulling out his gun from his shopping bag and taking aim at a petrified Rebecca. He fired the gun. "Why?...Why?" pleaded Rebecca after being shot by the same man who'd previously professed his love to her. Neighbours heard the screams and the gunshot. Bardo made his way up the street, running as fast as he could. Rebecca was quickly discovered lying on the floor wearing just a black bathrobe. She had wide, open eyes and was later pronounced dead at Cedars-Sinai Medical Center.

The LAPD issued a statement to reporters that same day, during which they mentioned that there was no record of her ever being harassed or a victim of an abusive fan. Likewise, studio security confirmed that none of the mail sent to Rebecca sounded menacing or had threatening undertones. Despite his odd behaviour on the studio lot, Bardo's obsession with Rebecca was seen as him merely being a lovestruck fan.

The day after her tragic murder, Tucson police were called about a strange man disrupting the traffic at a busy intersection. Bardo had been running frantically near a freeway, screaming and shouting that he'd murdered Rebecca Schaeffer, which ensured his swift arrest. Officers, perhaps initially dubious of his wild claims, found a picture of Rebecca in his pocket, resulting in them hastily contacting LA authorities. Police there were already aware of Bardo's strange behaviour; they'd received a call from a woman in Tennessee who told them Bardo was obsessed with Rebecca Schaeffer. Tucson police then faxed the suspect's mugshot to LAPD, who showed it to the victim's neighbours. They identified him as the same man who'd been scouring the area prior to her murder, asking people about Rebecca.

The Tennessee tipster turned out to be Bardo's sister, who told police of a troubling letter he sent her admitting to his obsession. In the letter, he stated, "I have to eliminate (the thing) that I cannot attain."

Before he sought out and murdered Rebecca, it was clear Bardo had problems. He accused his sibling of abusing him, and after threatening suicide, he was placed in a foster home. He once took himself off to Maine in a misguided search for Samantha Smith, a very young peace activist who'd been on the news after writing to Soviet leader Yuri Andropov (resulting in him inviting her to visit). After this episode, the teenager was placed back in foster care but ran away shortly after. This saw him spending a month in a psychiatric hospital to deal with his emotional problems. In 1985 he was discharged and bandied off to another foster home, a situation that didn't last long.

Samantha Smith sadly died in 1985 in a plane crash, aged just 13. This left Bardo needing a new source of obsession, leading him to turn his attention to singer and actress Debbie Gibson. He headed to New York in an unsuccessful attempt to meet her, just like his previous jaunt to Maine to track Samantha down. While there, Bardo took a trip to the place where Mark Chapman murdered John Lennon in 1980. Just like Chapman did, Bardo carried his coveted copy of *The Catcher in the Rye* with him when he sought out and coldy shot his victim.

He was inspired to hire an investigator to track Rebecca down from reading an article about criminal Arthur Richard Jackson, who was behind bars for stabbing actress Theresa Saldana in 1982 outside her property. In this eerily similar case, Jackson used a private investigator to find out where his victim lived. He was also in the US illegally - he was originally from Scotland and had already been deported twice. He tried to buy himself a gun but was unable to due to not having an American driver's license, so he carried out the attack with a knife. Fortunately, a delivery man caught Jackson mid-attack and pulled him off the terrified actress.

While in jail, Bardo said that "there was something very special" about Rebecca, noting that he was unable to shake his obsession: "I just couldn't let go of her," he would say.

Prosecutor Marcia Clark was tasked with the case, and almost straight away, she agreed not to seek a death sentence since Bardo waived his right to a jury trial. The case served up a cold dose of reality to not only the rich and famous but to anyone who heard it. It made people confront the idea that anyone you upset, aggravate or reject could track you down via the DMV, obtain your address and turn up at your house with malicious intentions in mind. These days, it's unheard of that a Hollywood celebrity, no matter how up and coming they are, would open their door to a complete stranger and engage in small talk.

The psychiatrist who interviewed Robert Bardo in jail said that he believed Bardo had been schizophrenic since he was a young child, but he didn't fit the definition of legal insanity. Bardo also told his psychiatrist that he was also inspired by the U2 song "Exit" from the album *Joshua Tree*. The song was inspired by Norman Mailer's novel, *The Executioner's Song*, a book about serial killer Gary Gilmore. The song was played in court a number of times. The lyrics were chilling given the context:

Hand in the pocket,

Finger on the steel,

The pistol weighed heavy,

His heart he could feel.

As the track was played in court, it seemed to evoke an odd reaction in Bardo. Despite being on trial for a horrific murder, the song perked him up; he visibly banged on his knees as if they were drums and lip-synced along with the words. Aside from this strange episode, he would sit looking sombre.

Bardo's attorney, Stephen Galindo, put forward that his client wasn't mentally well enough to be able to plan the crime he committed, arguing that he was only guilty of second-degree murder if anything. He told the court that Robert Bardo - like Rebecca Schaeffer - was a victim. Except, Bardo was a victim of a poor upbringing, let down by everyone he sought refuge in. He was a failure of the system, and he hadn't received the mental health care he required when it was obvious he wasn't of sound mind.

Superior Court Judge Dino Fulgoni sided with the prosecution's argument that Bardo wasn't insane, and on October 29, 1991, he was convicted of first-degree murder. The sentence was issued with the special circumstance of Bardo lying in wait. In December 1991, he was handed life in prison without the possibility of parole.

He's still behind bars in California at Avenal State Prison.

Still, there was the aftermath to deal with for Rebecca's friends and family. Rebecca's former agent said during a *20/20* interview that although he lost a good friend, "Hollywood lost a rising star, and the world lost an angel." Her father, Benson Schaeffer, recalled the last time he ever spoke to his daughter, and it was the day before her upcoming *Godfather* audition. She'd promised to call him after she'd been on set and let him know how it went. She was stripped of that opportunity.

With Rebecca's death being an unbearable loss for her family and friends, including her boyfriend, film director Brad Silberling, the circumstances of her murder also shook Hollywood. Rebecca's death caused those who dealt with fame to be more diligent, but those with unhealthy obsessions towards celebrities are still a problem for those in the limelight. Despite their abundance of security, Keanu Reeves, Sandra Bullock and Jennifer Aniston have all dealt with stalkers, some of whom have even entered their properties. They have been arrested for their harassing patterns of behaviour, which could have served as a deterrent for Bardo in his overzealous following of Rebecca.

Sadly, it wasn't until after her murder that stalking was classed as a crime. Eventually, in 1994, Congress agreed to pass the Driver's Privacy Protection Act, which required all states to restrict the information freely available from the DMV.

Rebecca wasn't wildly famous at the time of her death, but her unimaginable fate sees her frozen in time as a young, talented actress on the verge of big things. The heights she could've risen to remain unknown, all because an obsessive fan had the cunning to find out where she lived and the means to do so. If nothing else, when Hollywood talks of Rebecca Schaeffer, they remember how deadly fame can be and just how important it is to be wise to the prospect that some people are just dangerous when feelings are hurt, celebrity or not.

The Most Infamous Unsolved Hollywood Murder

On the mid-morning of January 15, 1947, Betty Bersinger and her daughter were taking a walk in Leimert Park, South LA, when something in the corner of her eye piqued her interest. Upon further inspection of the weedy area that caught her attention, she was confronted with a most horrific sight. A naked woman, cut in half at the waist, was lying rotting in the foliage as the Californian sun rose. Her paleness was offset by jet her black hair. Her face had been brutally deformed; whoever did this had slit her mouth open, with fleshy gashes running from ear to ear, possibly while she was still alive. She'd been tortured and mutilated; that was abundantly clear. In an act of malicious cruelty, the tattoo of a rose she had on her thigh had been sliced off and placed in her vagina.

Despite her state of shock and panic at the disturbing find, Betty immediately ran to a neighbour's house and called the police. Her understandably hysteric call ignited a frenzy among the LAPD, spanning over a number of divisions. As soon as the newspapers heard the shocking news, so did the rest of Los Angeles, sparking the beginning of the intrigue into the country's most famous - and still unsolved - murder cases.

A subsequent autopsy revealed the young victim had died after going into shock and haemorrhaging from concussion and her horrific facial lacerations. Her murder was undeniably, barbarically brutal and the young woman was no doubt terrified in her final moments.

The victim needed to be identified to help piece the shocking case together. An editor who worked for the *Examiner* offered up the idea of sending her fingerprints via an early fax machine (then named "Soundphoto") to Washington, D.C., where the FBI could then try and find a match. It didn't take them long. By January 16, authorities had identified the victim: Elizabeth Short, a 22-year-old who'd once been arrested for drinking while underage. The successful match meant police could inform Elizabeth's mother in Massachusetts of her daughter's death, as well as speak to her to gain more information about the young woman - except the newspapers spoke with her before the police had a chance to.

The cruel reporter from the Los Angeles Examiner called Phoebe Short up and congratulated her for Elizabeth's recent win in a beauty contest. This heartless lie helped the reporter coax information from Phoebe about her daughter. He asked, and the proud mother willingly told. Once the man found out everything he wanted to know, he informed the woman that her daughter hadn't actually won a beauty competition - she'd, in fact, been murdered. The cruel call gave the newspapers the young woman's entire life story, which helped them pad out the plethora of articles they were publishing about her.

On July 29, 1924, Elizabeth Short was born in Boston, Massachusetts, the middle of five daughters. As a teenager, she suffered severe asthma attacks and terrible bouts of bronchitis, so she underwent lung surgery to help her respiratory problems. After this, doctors advised the teen to be sure to live in a milder place during winter to avoid further breathing issues, so she lived in Miami every winter with family friends. She dropped out of high school in search of something different to the life she was expected to lead. In 1942, she headed to California to live with her estranged father. She'd not seen him since she was six but reconnected once again when she was 18, although the reunion didn't last long.

By January 1943, she'd moved out due to numerous arguments with her father. Needing to make a living, she found work at the Base Exchange at Camp Cooke, drifting from friends house to friends house, at one point living with a sergeant who allegedly beat her. By mid-1943, she'd moved on again, this time floating around Santa Barbara. Here, she was arrested in a local bar for underage drinking, meaning she was fingerprinted for her minor misdemeanour, which would later be used to successfully identify her after her murder. After this, she was supposed to return to live with her mother, but she detoured to Florida instead. Carefree, free-spirited and with a desire to seek more for her life, Elizabeth felt Florida was a reasonable substitute for Hollywood.

While here, she was introduced to Major Matthew Michael Gordon, Jr., a successful Army Air Force officer. The relationship was serious enough for Gordon to propose, but he would sadly die from injuries from a plane crash before the pair wed.

Elizabeth returned to Los Angeles in the summer of 1946, spending the last months of her life on Hollywood Boulevard in a rented room behind a nightclub, living out a real-life film-noir. Posthumously, Elizabeth was described as an up-and-coming actress, although this has been disputed. While she did harbour a desire to be an actress - as a lot of women in Hollywood did

- she had no acting credits assigned to her name. In death, she's permanently frozen in time as a young Hollywood starlet destined for the big screen, although this narrative is perhaps more a means of selling newspapers than it is reflective of the truth.

The investigation into her death initially centred around Long Beach, where those that knew Elizabeth affectionately called her *The Black Dahlia*, a play on words from the film *The Blue Dahlia*, a playful way of acknowledging her taste in black clothing. This name would become synonymous with Elizabeth and her tragic and brutal murder.

The Killer Sends Taunts

Police were seemingly making some headway in the case when they arrested Robert Manley, a married salesman who met Elizabeth shortly before her death, giving her a lift to the Biltmore Hotel on January 9. This was the last time she was seen. The suspect later positively identified one of Elizabeth's shoes and her purse found near her dead body, but he had alibis confirming he was nowhere near the crime scene when the victim was murdered. Subsequently, he was cleared of any involvement and released.

Towards the end of January, an ominous envelope emblazoned with the cut-out words *"Heaven is Here*!" was delivered to the Examiner's office. The contents included Elizabeth's personal items, including her birth certificate and her address book with the name "Mark Hansen" written on the cover. Police were tasked with tracking down the men named in the book and successfully found approximately 75 of them, most of whom admitted to meeting Elizabeth, albeit briefly. Their new person of interest, Mark Hansen, was tracked down and told police that the young woman had been sleeping at his place, which sounded right to police who were compiling their profile of Elizabeth as a drifter. He was soon dismissed as a suspect, however.

It didn't take too long for the authorities to be inundated with copycat letters from the supposed killer, often finding themselves sitting listening to fake confessions from men who wailed that they'd been the one to slice The Black Dahlia's face up. They also followed up on other possibly linked crimes, like the "Red Lipstick Murder" where the victim was violently stomped to death in February 1947. Despite some similarities, police couldn't find any real leads. Things were getting desperate.

The following year, a new lead surfaced. Leslie Dillon, who once resided in LA but was then living in Florida, called the police to tell them about someone he knew who may be Elizabeth's killer. However, police suspected it was Dillion who was the real killer and that he had split personalities. LAPD used their "Gangster Squad" to try and obtain a confession from the man, but this (illegal) plan was foiled when he made a note of his abduction and flung it out of a window. Police then investigated the man who he'd told them was the real killer, and he turned out to be innocent.

The Infamous Murder is Now Popular in Modern Media

For years, Elizabeth Short's murder files collected dust and people were no longer invested in the case. With no culprit caught - not even a suspect in sight - The Black Dahlia case remained untouched. However, as time went by, the literary world took a renewed interest in the cold case. Based on the killing, fiction books were penned, like John Gregory Dunne's *True Confessions* and James Ellroy's *The Black Dahlia*. Non-fiction books followed, with Janice Knowlton's 1995 *Daddy Was the Black Dahlia Killer*.

Steve Hodel, a former detective with LAPD, also aired his take on the crime in his offering, *Black Dahlia Avenger: The True Story (2003)*, covering the fact his dad, George, was once a suspect in the case. More books have been released, with each author trying to crack the case with their own hypothesis and theories, including a conspiracy against Leslie Dillon and the notion of an LAPD cover-up.

Other theories include that the killer was Mark Hansen, the man with whom she'd stayed just prior to her murder and whose name was written on her address book. There were rumours that the older man was fixated on Elizabeth and that the young woman had rejected his advances. Some researchers suggest that Hansen and Leslie Dillon were in cahoots; after all, Dillon knew way more about the murder than any other member of the public. When he was arrested by police initially, they remained coy about the information they gave him about the crime, but he offered up knowledge only someone involved in the crime would know.

Pie Eatwell, in her book *Black Dahlia, Red Rose*, proposes that Hansen acquired Dillion to kill Elizabeth after she rebuffed him.

She believes Elizabeth was murdered in the Aster Motel, where Dillon had been staying and where the owners of the establishment admitted finding one of their cabins stained with blood and covered in faecal matter on January 15; the same day Elizabeth was found.

Witnesses staying at the hotel also recall seeing a girl who resembled Elizabeth Short - she had striking black hair and pale skin, so was memorable. Alongside this woman, they described a man who fit the physical traits of Mark Hansen. It's been suggested that the crime was covered up by the police due to Mark Hansen's connections with LAPD.

While certain arguments and theories are convincing, sadly it's unlikely we'll ever truly know who brutally murdered Elizabeth Short. With a lack of enduring evidence, and the case's key witnesses deceased, there's nothing but hearsay and circumstantial evidence remaining. Whichever way you want to look at it, despite heavy clues that appeared to point to their involvement in the murder, neither Leslie Dillon nor Mark Hansen was ever arrested for The Black Dahlia killers. Although some people may find it peculiar that years later, Dillon would name his daughter "Elizabeth."

The Hollywood Ripper

The press gave him many names, such as "The Chiller Killer" and "The Boy Next Door Killer"; however, one name stuck more than the others: "The Hollywood Ripper". The police had long suspected the identity of the killer who lurked in Los Angeles before he was eventually brought to justice. Before being apprehended, The Ripper violently murdered two women, attempted to kill a third, and possibly murdered a fourth at some point during his spree.

Michael Thomas Gargiulo was born in 1976, growing up in Glenview, Illinois, a quiet suburb nestled in northwest Chicago. He claimed to have suffered abuse from his father and his seven siblings while growing up, although his claims were never validated. The young boy had a reputation as something of a bully around the otherwise calm village, having a short fuse with his peers. Even his friends had to acknowledge his quick temper. Gargiulo would bewilder them with his ability to go from calm to crazy in record time, and when he flipped, they'd refer to his outburst as "inhuman."

Not far from Gargiulo's childhood home lived the Pacaccio's. Doug Pacaccio was friends with Michael Gargiulo, with both of them attending Glenbrook South High School. Doug's sister, Tricia, also went to the same high school, graduating in 1993 and planning on heading to university later that year. On August 13, 1993, the teen went to meet her former classmates for dinner and to catch up before they all went their separate ways and headed to university. After a fun evening, Tricia came back home just after midnight.

Just a few short hours later, her father opened his front door to the worst sight imaginable; his 18-year-old daughter, doused in her own blood, laying on the steps outside. She'd been stabbed a dozen times and endured a broken arm from the vicious attack. There were traces of DNA under the teenager's fingernails, but forensic technology was still very limited at the time, and a suspect wasn't found from the samples.

Just two days before, Michael Gargiulo had given Tricia a lift to her friend's house, which made him a person of interest for police to speak to. While authorities questioned him, he vehemently denied any wrongdoing and even implicated another teen from the area. There was no evidence to proceed with an arrest, and no charges were ever filed against the boy Gargiulo had suggested was responsible for the crime. The case turned cold.

In 1995, a woman came forward to report that Gargiulo had raped her. She was just 17 at the time and told police that she'd just ended a relationship with her rapist. Despite breaking up, she wished to remain friends with Gargiulo and was still visiting him socially. On this particular visit, she said Gargiulo bound her tightly with handcuffs, forced her pants off, and raped her. She was so terrified she couldn't move.

The brutish teenager was also involved in an incident at Glenbrook South High School and was apprehended while attempting to break into unlocked cars. He was handed 18-month probation and fined $200.

As the millennium dawned, Gargiulo followed in his brother's footsteps and made his way to LA. The visibly fit and athletic young man had trained extensively in martial arts and boxing, so he found it easy to land a job as a bouncer at a popular bar on Sunset Boulevard. Here, he made friends with his co-workers, two other bouncers who found Gargiulo somewhat a fantasist but harmless. Anthony DiLorenzo and Temer Leary, his two new bouncer buddies, and Gargiulo were cruising around Los Angeles one afternoon in 2000 when Gargiulo said something disturbing,

"You guys ever killed anybody?" he asked the two men sitting in the car. When they just looked at each other, Gargiulo carried on, "I have. I buried a bitch. I left the bitch on the steps for dead."

With Gargiulo being renowned for his elaborate lies and unbelievable exaggerations, the two men brushed off his claims as another one of his fantastical tales. They didn't get in touch with police about his abrupt confession until after he'd been arrested for the Hollywood Ripper murders. Gargiulo didn't manage to keep his job on Sunset Boulevard for too long - he was fired for punching a customer and subsequently took on jobs as a repairman.

Later that year, he met and became fast friends with Ashley Ellerin, a fashion student who lived close to him in Hollywood. Gargiulo quickly became infatuated with the 22-year-old, coming by her place at all hours and even sitting outside in his car in the middle of the night. Perhaps he was checking to see if she had any dates visiting her. She'd dated some young up and comers in Hollywood, including Vin Diesel and Aston Kutcher, whose successes overshadowed Gargiulo's. His perpetual turning up at her house and offerings to fix things didn't match what these movie stars could; glamour, excitement and a gateway to Hollywood.

On February 21, 2001, Ashley was expecting Kutcher to come to pick her up for a date at a Grammy Awards party. The actor was late getting to her house, arriving at 11 pm, much later than their agreed-upon time. He knocked on the door a few times, and when he didn't get a reply, peeked through the window to see if she was there, thinking she was maybe angry at him for not turning up on time. When he looked in the house, he saw spilt wine stains all over the floor, which he assumed was from the party Ashley had hosted a few nights prior. Thinking his date had gone out without him, he left.

What Kutcher didn't know was that the wine was, in fact, blood, and as he was knocking on the door, his girlfriend was lying dead inside. She'd been stabbed a total of 47 times violently, some of the wounds going as deep as 6 inches, including one that saw the attacker nearly severing Ashley's head from her body.

After speaking to those close to Ashley, LAPD detectives set out looking for the man her friends called "Mike the furnace man." It wasn't long before they got a name and a driver's license picture. The furnace man was Michael Gargiulo.

By a stroke of good luck, the cold case division at Cook County Sheriff's department was in the process of re-examining the evidence they'd collected from the Tricia Pacaccio murder years earlier. They ran the DNA they'd gathered from underneath her fingernails through their systems and rechecked everyone who'd been in contact with her in the days before she was killed. This shortlist of people included Gargiulo. In 2002, detectives from Cook County flew to LA and told the LAPD about their need to find and speak to Gargiulo. The LA police department was able to help straight away, showing Cook County police Gargiulo's driver's licence photo, asking them if that was the guy they were looking for. It was - and both police forces confirmed they were tracking this man as a potential murder suspect.

Gargiulo was eventually apprehended, but he didn't give up without a fight, struggling with arresting detectives before eventually having his DNA sample taken in a hospital emergency room. His DNA matched the evidence found under Tricia's fingernails.

The Police Have Evidence Tying Gargiulo to the Murder... But He Was Still Set Free

However, the attorney's office in Cook County put a halt to indicting Gargiulo as they argued his DNA could have been on the victim through normal contact. The killer was free to roam the streets of LA, seeing as the LAPD had no tangible, physical evidence that Gargiulo murdered Ashley Ellerin, either - just pure circumstantial evidence.

Chillingly, a former girlfriend of Gargiulo alleged that in 2003, he violently attacked her, assaulting her relentlessly, punching her in the face and shouting threats to murder her. She said he told her he'd get away with the killing due to his "extensive knowledge" of police forensics. Gargiulo thought he'd gotten away with murder and had no qualms that he'd get away with it again. Before that incident, the two had become acquainted while he fixed her air conditioning unit, where he begged the shocked woman to go out with him while wearing his dirty work overalls and blue disposable shoe covers. While she agreed, he became obsessive quickly, stalking her to the point she filed a restraining order against him.

In 2005, Gargiulo met another woman and lived with her in El Monte, Los Angeles. On the other side of their apartment lived 32-year-old Maria Bruno, a recently single mother of four young children. She became Gargiulo's new obsession. On December 1, 2005, after a short time stalking his victim, The Hollywood Ripper struck again, climbing through Maria's kitchen window while she was fast asleep. He violently attacked the vulnerable woman, stabbing her relentlessly and slashing her throat. He also cut off her breasts, disturbingly placing one of them over her mouth.

She was only discovered when her ex-husband, who had custody of their children, went to see her and walked in on the horrifying murder scene. Police found one clue - a single blue disposable shoe cover just outside Maria's apartment.

Likely feeling like he was unstoppable, Gargiulo quickly moved on to his next victim after moving to Santa Monica. Across the backstreet from his apartment lived 27-year-old Michelle Murphy, a petite woman who Gargiulo swiftly saw as prey. He even had a perfect view of her bedroom from his apartment, which he utilised numerous times before attacking her.

On April 28, 2008, Michelle was awakened by a most horrific ordeal - a man, with his face almost completely covered by a cap and hood, was repeatedly stabbing her in the chest. Despite her small frame and nasty injuries, the brave woman fought him off. He eventually scuttled out of the door, telling his victim, "I'm sorry," before fleeing. Gargiulo cut himself on his knife during the senseless attack as Michelle struggled with him for the blade, leaving his DNA at the scene. The Santa Monica Police Department ran the evidence through a national database, bringing up a match: Gargiulo's DNA sample from when he was a suspect in the Pacaccio case.

He was finally arrested for attempted murder in June 2008, and his bail was set at $1.1 million. A subsequent search of his car found his bag of tools and the blue disposable shoe slippers he was so fond of wearing. A search of his previous apartment in El Monte uncovered the matching disposable shoe he wore during the murder of Maria Bruno. A DNA swab taken from this matched Gargiulo, conclusively pinning him to the crime scene.

He was charged with the cold-blooded murders of both Ashley Ellerin and Maria Bruno in September 2008 and also faced allegations of lying in wait for his unsuspecting victims.

It took three more agonising years before the prosecutors from Cook County were confident enough that they had strong enough evidence to proceed and charge Gargiulo. In July 2011, after his long reign of terror in Hollywood, Michael Gargiulo was charged with fatally stabbing Tricia Pacaccio almost a decade before in 1993.

The trial in California began in May 2019, with Gargiulo being called a "serial sexual-thrill killer" by prosecutors who described him as a sadistic killer who enjoyed slaughtering attractive young women. There were hundreds of witnesses called to the stand, one of whom was Ashton Kutcher, who had to recount the evening he went to Ashley Ellerin's place to pick her up for a date, only for her to have been killed just hours before he turned up. Kutcher spoke of how, when he found out she'd been murdered, he went straight to police because his fingerprints were all over the front door and window.

The defence team for Gargiulo protested his innocence in horrific slayings and stated he had "no recollection" of attacking Michelle Murphy due to his mental illness. The jury saw through the weak argument and he was found guilty on all charges, with the recommendation that he be put to death for his crimes. Currently, the death sentence in California is suspended. He is due, as of 2021, to be extradited back to Illinois for the murder of Tricia Pacaccio.

While this case is akin to a slasher movie script, with Michelle Murphy being the "final girl" who finally brought the killer to justice, it's a frightening thought that people like Gargiulo walk among us. This case, for me, shows that anything Hollywood can conjure up in a horror movie is nowhere near as terrifying as what evil people in real life are capable of.

The Son of a Hollywood Icon

Christian Brando was born in Los Angeles on May 11, 1958, to actress Anna Kashfi and screen icon Marlon Brando. Hollywood legend Marlon would be known for many things over the course of his life: movies like *A Streetcar Named Desire*, his standout performance in *The Godfather*, and his colourful personal life. Another thing that would bring controversy to the Brando name would be from his son, Christian, who fatally shot his sister's boyfriend.

Marlon Brando met Anna Kashfi in 1955, who became pregnant in 1957. The pair tied the knot in 1958, although Marlon would later state that he'd only agreed to the marriage because Anna was pregnant with his child and admitted that throughout the marriage he had other relationships. The marriage ended a year after Christian was born.

Christian was subsequently passed between his mother and father, with his parents becoming more and more hostile and aggressive towards each other. The young boy was often witness to the abuse his parents inflicted upon each other, at one point being left alone in his mother's car while she attacked Marlon Brando in his Wilshire Boulevard office, raining blows on him with her fists.

Anna and Marlon were embroiled in a lengthy custody battle, which his father eventually won when Christian was 13. Prior to this, his mother had taken the young boy out of school and taken him to Mexico with her.

However, Christian's new life with his father wasn't much more stable. Marlon wasn't very involved in his son's life, spending little time with him and paying nannies to take care of Christian. Despite the extravagance and abundance of wealth surrounding him, the teenager remained blasé about the world he was now a part of. He would flit between living on his dad's private island located close to Tahiti and his lavish Hollywood home on Laurel Canyon. Anything he wanted was his - except the attention he craved from his father.

Christian was all too aware of his dad's numerous relationships with multiple women, some of whom he fathered children with. Speaking of this time years later, Christian said he'd "sit down at the breakfast table and say, 'Who are you?'" when his dad brought a new fling home.

It looked like Christian may follow in his father's footsteps after he had two minor acting roles in comedy *The Secret Life of an American Wife* and romcom *I Love You, Alice B. Toklas!* with Peter Sellers, both released when the youngster was 10 in 1968. He also had parts in four other productions, although he chose to frequently be credited as "Gary Brown" between 1980 and 1990, perhaps to step away from the surname that preceded him. However, his chaotic personal life would put a damper on that idea; specifically, the act of violence he carried out on May, 16, 1990, that resulted in the death of another man.

Christian's younger half-sister Cheyenne was in a long-term relationship with Dag Drollet and was pregnant with his unborn child. The pair had come to LA from Tahiti to visit Cheyenne's side of the family, despite the fact that she was heavily pregnant.

(As a side note, she gave birth to a son named Tuki, who goes by Tuki Brando and went on to have a successful modelling career). Dag, Cheyenne, and her mother were all lodging at Marlon's luxurious place on Mulholland Drive as the blended family caught up with one another. Although Cheyenne had been in a relationship with Dag for almost four years, and despite Marlon being friendly with the Drollet's for many years, Christian had never met his soon to be brother-in-law until that evening of May 16. It would also be the night he would shoot Dag Drollet to death.

On that cool May evening, Christian and his sister dined together at classic Hollywood eatery, Musso & Frank Grill, where Cheyenne told her protective older brother that Dag had been assaulting her, claims which have never been corroborated. Christian would later recall his sister telling him this, saying, "She went off on this bizarre tangent." True or not, her description of an abusive relationship left Christian enraged. To quell his anger, he would take to drinking alcohol, but this could only subdue his outrage for so long. By the time 11 pm rolled around, Christian was back at the Brando residence and ready to confront his sister's abuser. Armed with a gun, he took himself to the living room to demand answers from Dag, and in his own words, just wanted to "scare him." Instead, he shot him in cold blood. Cheyenne was in another room when the gun went off, which happened, Christian said, as the pair were struggling in a physical altercation.

Robert Shapiro, a lawyer who was part of the team who successfully defended O.J Simpson (another tale of Hollywood murder) was also appointed to defend Christian Brando.

Christian was charged with murder, but the prosecution team weren't able to proceed with the charge due to Cheyenne - a key witness for them - not being contactable or offering up her testimony. While the trial was taking place, Cheyenne had been admitted into a psychiatric hospital by Marlon after her erratic and troublesome behaviour escalated. Despite a number of attempts to get Cheyenne to visit California to testify (in spite of her poor mental state), a judge went ahead and demanded all efforts to get her testimony to be stopped.

Christian went on to plead guilty to manslaughter and served his time behind bars, eventually getting released in 1996. We'll never truly know whether what happened that night was murder or manslaughter. The only person who could answer that conundrum is Christian himself; did he carry that gun with intent, or did a struggle cause the gun to go off like he said? The answer to this is something he took to his grave in January 2008, when a lethal bout of pneumonia took his life at the age of 49.

Cheyenne wouldn't recover from her mental health problems and sadly committed suicide at the age of 25, one year before her brother got out of jail.

However, there's more to Brando's story. Christian, like his father, had a colourful personal life, and the murder of Dag Drollet wouldn't be the only murder he would be accused of. Robert Blake claimed that Christian Brando was complicit in the 2001 murder of his wife, Bonnie Lee Bakley.

MURDERS IN HOLLYWOOD: TRUE CRIME STORIES OF HOMICIDE IN THE HILLS

Bonnie was known to be "obsessed" with celebrities, and even her family attested to her obsession for those who were famous. Taped phone calls would reveal that Bonnie was adamant she was going to marry someone famous, as it enabled her to "feel better" than other people. She moved to LA in the early 90s to pursue her dream man. Here, she chased a number of famous men, but her efforts were often in vain. She was always interested in Christian Brando, but nothing ever materialised with them until he was released from jail in '96. By 1999, she'd fallen pregnant and was insistent that Christian was the child's father, so much so she named her Christian Shannon Brando. However, she was also dating Robert Blake during this period, and after a DNA test, it was proven the child was his. Her name was subsequently changed to Rose. The pair wed in November 2000.

Still, by all accounts, Bonnie was still insisting that Christian was the father of her child, a claim that enraged Brando. A recorded conversation between the pair exposed Christian as being verbally abusive towards the woman, stating, "You're lucky. Not on my behalf, but you're lucky someone ain't out there to put a bullet in your head."

This didn't bode well when Bonnie was found dead with a bullet hole in her head, sitting up in Blake's car. Both men were suspects; both had motives to kill her.

Pre-trial hearings in the case saw Christian being implicated in the murder, offering the rationale that and he had the exact same motives as Robert Blake to kill Bonny Lee Bakley. Bonnie was dating both men at the same time. Letters from Bonnie to Robert exposed possible financial motives for her pursuit of both men. She told each man that they were her child's father. Christian was on the birth certificate. Mere days before her murder, Bonnie sent photos of the baby to Christian whom she continued to claim was the father. This angered him and caused him to lash out in the recorded phone call where he stated she was lucky someone hadn't put a "bullet in her head yet."

Christian was, in fact, in Washington state on the night of Bonnie's death, something which was corroborated. It was alleged that Robert had arranged for some associates to carry out the murder, one associate in particular: Hollywood stunt man, Duffy Hambleton. He alleged that the jilted husband tried to procure him to carry out the hit on his wife. The stunt man said he refused the murder-for-cash offer.

Robert Blake denied this. He admitted to knowing Duffy but said it was because he hired him to act as a personal security guard as he and Bonnie were victims of a stalker. Pre-trial testimony, however, alleged that Duffy was an associate of Christian and that *he* was the one who organised the murder of Bonnie to gain the friendship of Brando. The judge, however, halted the defence from mentioning that during the trial.

Christian was called as a witness during Robert Blake's trial but would refuse to offer a testimony, invoking his Fifth Amendment constitutional rights. His actions in court ensured he was in contempt of court charge and conviction.

In the end, Robert Blake was found liable for the murder of his wife, Bonnie Lee Bakley.

Christian was also accused of being violent to his wife, Deborah Presley (who claimed to be Elvis Presley's illegitimate daughter.) In 2005, he was charged with two counts of spousal abuse and pleaded guilty to both of them. He was given three years probation and had to attend drug and alcohol treatment.

Deborah stated that her former husband repeatedly sexually assaulted her and forced her into sexual acts by threatening to kill her or chop her young daughter up "into a million pieces". These claims were heard in court, although the pair managed to settle the accusations out of court in 2007. He would be dead the following January, taking the truth of all of his alleged crimes with him.

The Wonderland Murders

8763 Wonderland Avenue, Los Angeles: despite the dreamy name, this was in fact a well-known drug house in the area. Situated high above the notorious Sunset Strip, the infamous property often hosted the seedy side of LA and the wannabes that were passing through. It was home to hundreds of thousands of dollars worth of illegal drugs, guns and stolen items and would go on to become the scene of a violent and bloody mass murder. On July 1, 1981, the lifeless bodies of four people were discovered at the Wonderland residence, all of them beaten mercilessly.

The Wonderland Avenue house was the Wonderland Gang's base and a place where they distributed their ample supply of drugs. Throughout the '70s, they were Los Angeles' most successful distributor of a new 'it' drug - cocaine. Their illegal operation grew exponentially over the course of a few years.

The house was leased under the name Joy Miller, although the property was home to a whole cast of people, many of whom stayed for a while but eventually left to seek pastures new. Joy was a heroin addict, although things hadn't always been this way for her. She'd fallen into the wrong crowd - the Wonderland crowd - after divorcing her wealthy husband and upping sticks from her luxurious Beverly Hills home.

Her new boyfriend was called Billy Deverell, and he was a high ranking member of the Wonderland Gang. He would be made out to be a reluctant member of the gang by the media, a man who wasn't proud of his drug abuse and run-ins with the law, but one who struggled to find honest work after his string of convictions. The press wouldn't be as sympathetic to the gang's leader, however. Ron Launius was a criminal kingpin who ran various illegal businesses and he was someone most people wouldn't want to mess with. Launius began his criminal enterprise during his time in the Vietnam War, which saw him dishonourably discharged after he was caught smuggling drugs into the US, concealed in the dead bodies of US servicemen.

Launius seemed destined for a life of crime. This nefarious lifestyle could have been nipped in the bud if he was handed the life sentence he was due for killing a man years prior. He only avoided life in jail when the prosecution's main witness died in an accident. Police knew Launius wasn't able to fly under the radar for long and knew they'd most certainly be seeing him again. By 1981, he was a person of interest in over twenty other murders.

Susan, Launius's wife, also resided at the Wonderland house. Just like her spouse, she was an avid drug taker, although she did refrain from partaking in any of the violence and criminal behaviour the rest of the gang indulged in. While Susan wasn't someone you'd pinpoint as being affiliated with a deadly gang, neither were some of the other Wonderland residents and regulars. Famous pornographer, John Holmes, was a frequent visitor and often bought - or borrowed - cocaine from the gang.

While it was lucrative, cocaine wasn't the only way the Wonderland gang made their money. Heroin was also a good cash cow, as well as a personal preference of many of the group's members. Another side hustle of theirs was an armed robbery gig, and the gang would even steal from their drug-pushing competitors to kick them out of the race. However, this was only effective for a while, and it would soon come back to bite them in a brutal way.

A few days prior to the Wonderland gang slayings, members of the crew broke into and robbed the house of their rival gang leader, Eddie Nash, who was a restauranteur, club owner, and all-around criminal bad guy.

Ron Launius and Billy Deverell planned the burglary. They donned police disguises and went with fellow crew members David Lind and Tracy McCourt to Eddie's home, where they forcefully subdued him and handcuffed him, as well as his bodyguard, Gregory Diles. Partway through the robbery, while Eddie was being forced to open his safe full of drugs and money, Lind shot Diles unintentionally, wounding him, although not fatally. Despite the mistake, the group walked away from their rival's home totally unrecognised, with a staggering $1.2 million worth of drugs, cash, jewellery, and guns. Ironically, the guns were part of a collection of firearms the Wonderland gang had sold Eddie Nash a few days earlier.

Police were unable to identify a suspect initially, although Nash was able to pinpoint a few people he strongly suspected. The top of his suspect list was John Holmes. His behaviour on the day of the robbery-gone-wrong was strange; he came to the house three separate times that morning, which Nash suspected was in order to ensure the patio door was open for the Wonderland henchmen to enter later that day.

Best known for being Liberace's former partner, Scott Thorson, was also a regular at Nash's house. He made claims that Eddie Nash was so confident Holmes was involved in the heist that he forced his (still badly-injured) bodyguard to find him and use violence to obtain the true assailants' names. Thorson's story has never been confirmed or denied, but it rings true since just days later the robbers were found brutally attacked in their Wonderland residence.

A Violent Retribution

On the mid-afternoon of July 1, 1981, police responded to the panicked phone call from a pair of removal men. They'd been doing their job at the property next door to 8763 Wonderland when they began to hear desperate pleas and moans coming from the infamous property. The investigators that arrived at the scene were greeted with a bloodbath.

The brutalised, bloody body of David Lind's girlfriend, Barbara Richardson, was found lying on the floor beside the couch she's been fast asleep on. She'd been accosted while she slept and was beaten to death.

Joy Miller was also beaten to death, most likely with the bloodied hammer found tangled in the bedsheets she still lay in. Her boyfriend, Deverell, slumped over at the foot of the bed, was sitting among the numerous metal pipes that littered the floor. In the next room, Ron Launius lay dead. His face was so bloodied, beaten and concave that he was unrecognisable despite his notoriety with the police.

His wife was discovered doused in her own blood on the floor next to the bed where her husband lay. Just like her spouse, Susan's skull had been violently bashed relentlessly. By some miracle, she was still alive - just. The pained pleas the removal men heard had been from a desperate Susan as she clung to life.

Although she survived the attack, she sustained brain damage that left her with permanent amnesia. This means she's got no recollection of the events that took place in 8763 Wonderland avenue on July 1.

The police searched the ransacked property and spoke with the neighbours, who admitted that they'd heard screams coming from next door around 3 am that morning. Since the house was renowned for being loud and housing people who exhibited drug-induced and disruptive behaviour, the neighbours assumed the same as they always did - that the Wonderland gang were partying and calling the cops wouldn't serve to quell any ruckus the gang were so prone to having.

Astonishingly, Susan Launius had been alive throughout the whole robbery-mass murder, bleeding out on the hard floor with a broken skull for over 12 agonising hours.

Subsequent searches of the property by police also found some potentially damning evidence: a clear, bloody handprint above the beaten body of Ron Launius. Upon further inspection, police were able to tie the print to John Holmes, who was quickly arrested and charged with the "Four on the Floor" murders (as they were now being dubbed). The prosecution insisted that

Holmes had turned hostile towards the Wonderland gang after being unfairly compensated in the division of the swag from the robbery of Eddie Nash's house.

However, the story didn't quite ring true. It's unusual to go from low-level criminal to mass murder, so it seemed more likely to both the jury and the public the adult film-star had merely been in the wrong place at the wrong time and was caught in the bloody crossfire. It turned out that Holmes was instead bribed with a promise of drugs by the Wonderland gang to go ensure easy access to Eddie Nash's place by unlocking the door. This job took Holmes a few trips, and his odd behaviour that day made him prime suspect to Nash.

Because of this, Nash's henchmen were sent to beat Holmes up until he would agree to let Nash's gang into the Wonderland property. It didn't take long for Holmes to be acquitted, but due to his refusal to give a shred of evidence during his trial, he served 110 days behind bars for contempt of court.

Police then had to tackle their new suspect: Eddie Nash.

They suspected he'd murdered members of the gang out of revenge, and after police questioned Nash for some time, they finally arrested the gang leader and charged him with plotting the barbaric murders. But, Nash was yet again saved from a life behind bars by a hung jury. One juror was the difference between Nash walking free or getting a guilty verdict. However, ever the perpetual criminal, Nash wouldn't remain a free man forever.

In 2000, he was charged with money laundering and drug trafficking. He agreed to a plea bargain, where he admitted to bribing the one objecting juror in his original trial.

As well as this revelation, he also confessed to sending his henchmen to repossess his stolen money, jewellery and guns from the Wonderland house on the night of the murders, but he would never admit to ordering the violent murders.

The Wonderland slayings is one of the most gruesome crimes to occur in Hollywood, and the house itself is now a macabre tourist attraction for LA, and the house itself is part of an LA ghost tour.

The Tragic Scream Queen

If you're a horror movie fan, you'll likely recognise the name, Dominique Dunne. She's famous for her role in the 1982 classic horror *Poltergeist*. She was familiar with the Hollywood scene from a young age after she began acting in LA as a teen, and '82 seemed to be the year her career was eventually picking up some rapid momentum. Sadly, this was also the year she was cruelly murdered, meaning the 22-year-old would never get to realise the potential she so wanted to offer the world.

The beginning of the promising young stars' end was the year before, in 1981, at a party. Dominique was introduced to John Sweeney, who was working as a sous-chef at the celebrity hangout and restaurant *Ma Maison*. Just weeks after their first encounter, the pair moved in together into her West Hollywood apartment. It didn't take long for the honeymoon period to evaporate, however - Sweeney exposed his ugly side pretty quickly after they began living together. He was possessive, jealous and abusive. Unusually for an abuser, Sweeney made almost no attempt whatsoever to conceal the emotional and physical violence he inflicted upon Dominique, hurting her brazenly in front of her family and friends. At one point, Dominique sought refuge at her mothers home, but Sweeney turned up full of rage, hurling his fists on the doors and windows demanding that he be let in.

Dominique's dad also witnessed the clear signs of the toxic relationship when he visited his daughter in LA. He noted how Sweeney seemed far more invested in the relationship than

Dominique was. Not only that, he saw Sweeney attack a fan of Dominique's for merely being excited at meeting one of their heroes. The aggressive man shook the fan after they struck up a conversation with Dominique, despite the conversation being innocent, Sweeney's jealousy took over yet again.

Dominique's father met his daughter in a restaurant on a separate occasion and sat alone as he waited for the couple who were running awfully late. When they did show up, he could clearly see Dominique had been crying. The subsequent meal was uncomfortable for the group to endure, and the atmosphere was shrouded in nervousness from Dominique. All the while, Dominick Dunne was contemplating if his daughter was struggling to end the harmful relationship she was in.

Witnesses also saw Sweeney pulling chunks of Dominique's hair out, tugging her violently at the roots while screaming at her. Another friend witnessed what Dominique would describe herself as an "attempted murder" from Sweeney. The attack was so brutal that the friend heard "loud gagging sounds" coming from another room and raced in to see what was happening. They witnessed Dominique being attacked, but weasel-like Sweeney denied attempting to murder his girlfriend and swore to the concerned guest that everything was okay.

It was that night when Dominique fled the property through an open bathroom window and managed to jump in her car before Sweeney got to her, locking the doors to ensure her brutish boyfriend couldn't hurt her. Still, the crazed man flung himself onto the hood of the car in an attempt to get her to stay.

Regardless, Dominique drove off and escaped. This should have been the end of the toxic relationship, but Sweeney wouldn't let go of Dominique so easily.

The Young Actress Hopes for a Fresh Start

After this particularly violent incident, Dominique understandably refused to step back into the house where she'd endured bouts of violence at the hands of her abuser. She sought solace by staying with her mother and at various friends' properties. She made a phone call to Sweeney to formally break off the relationship. Sweeney eventually moved out of their shared property, allowing Dominique to move back in and have the locks replaced on the West Hollywood home. It seemed that she'd finally escaped the clutches of her abusive partner once and for all.

Dominique was getting on with life, and as the weeks went by was becoming more carefree and relaxed about her living situation. Work was still coming in at a steady rate, and a couple of weeks after moving back into her home, she was spending the afternoon rehearsing for an upcoming TV show with her co-star David Packer.

Jealous Sweeney rang her during this time but ended up at the residence just minutes after trying to speak to her on the phone. With a newfound assertiveness and sense of confidence, Dominique went to the door to speak to an angry Sweeney. Despite her reluctance to talk to him, he would cause a scene if she didn't step out on the porch to hear him out. David Packer remained indoors as his friend went out to speak with her ex. Unbeknown to him, Dominique was stepping out for the last time.

After a little while, Packer heard an argument erupt, and when he heard smacks, screams and thuds, he called the police. However, the authorities advised him that West Hollywood wasn't in their jurisdiction. Panicking and unsure of what to do next, Packer called a friend and stated that should Dominique be dead, Sweeney did it. Eventually, the actor mustered up the courage to venture outside, where he found Sweeney hovering over some bushes. Upon further inspection, he saw Dominique lying lifeless in the shrubbery, and Sweeney ordered a terrified Packer to call the police. This time, perhaps due to the severity of the crime, police showed up.

John Sweeney admitted to attempting to murder Dominique and planned to then kill himself.

Dominique was immediately sent to the nearest hospital, where she was rushed onto life support. However, there was no hope; the young actress was tragically brain dead and there was no choice but to eventually remove her from life support. She donated her kidneys and heart for transplant.

Sweeney was facing first-degree murder charges. He would later claim that he couldn't remember what he'd done, only that he'd fought with his ex then blacked out and regained awareness when he saw Dominique's lifeless body. The charges were subsequently changed to the less-serious one of voluntary manslaughter, of which he was eventually found guilty. John

Sweeney served just three and a half years behind bars for the cruel and senseless murder of rising star, Dominique Dunne. He's since changed his name.

This case is certainly frightening in that it can happen to any of us. Dominique Dunne was a young, bright, Hollywood actress and despite her fame and surrounding herself with friends and family, she was unable to truly escape the relentless chasing of her obsessive ex. The abusive man only stopped when he'd snuffed her out during what ought to have been some of the best years of her life.

The Hillside Strangler

The Hillside Strangler is the ominous name given to the duo who stalked the darkness of LA to kidnap, torture, rape, and murder young girls and women. While their given name suggests just the one Strangler, two men were actually behind the slayings: cousins Angelo Buono and Kenneth Bianchi. They are collectively still referred to as the 'Hillside Strangler" because initially, police were only searching for one culprit. It soon transpired that the person picking off women and dumping them in the hills wasn't working alone. The brutality and violence used by these two men towards their victims left not just California in a state of shock but made headlines around the world.

Angelo Buono, the elder of the two killer cousins, was born in New York in 1934. His Italian parents divorced when he was still very young, which prompted his mother to relocate to California when Buono was five. Although his upbringing wasn't exactly settled, there had been no real traumas in his young life that would explain his early obsession with rape. As a teen, he'd brag to his peers about the girls he'd raped. While other boys his age were idolising famous sportsmen like the boxer Sugar Ray Robinson, Buono looked up to Caryl Chessman, a perpetual criminal who was convicted of raping 17 women. Still, despite hero-worshipping the serial rapist, Buono analysed his rapes enough to pick holes in his technique; he believed his idol should have killed his victims.

Despite his alarmingly unhealthy views on sex and women, Buono got his high school sweetheart pregnant and married her. However, he swiftly left seventeen-year-old Geraldine Vinal no more than a week after their nuptials, leaving her to bring up their son alone. After the divorce was finalised, Buono flatly refused to pay a penny of child support for his child, who Geraldine named Michael. Buono would go on to marry Mary Castillo, going on to father five more children with her.

Various sources have reported that in 1964, Buono raped his two-year-old daughter Grace, but there's not enough verified information or evidence to confirm such a horrific event occurred. However, with Buono's penchant for raping young girls and his warped views on sex, it certainly wouldn't have been out of the realms of possibility.

His marriage to Mary Castillo also disintegrated in 1964 after she made claims he abused her both sexually and physically, although, despite this, she tried to repair their marriage not long after leaving him. The desire to reconcile was one-sided, however; Buono handcuffed his estranged wife and threatened her with a gun, an event that saw her drop her mission to get back with him. Despite his average looks, lack of paternal instincts towards his children, and poor treatment of the opposite sex, Buono managed to build up a reputation as something of a ladies' man.

In 1965, he married a third time to Nannette Campino, with whom he had two more children. Nannette also had children from another marriage. During this union, Buono was caught stealing cars and subsequently sentenced to a year behind bars.

However, due to his abundance of young children, the judge suspended this sentence so he could work to earn money to support his offspring. Nannette, like the rest of the women who entered into a relationship with Buono, would eventually leave him in 1971 due to his sexual and physical abuse of her. It's also alleged that Buono raped her daughter during their marriage, although the information available about this isn't enough to corroborate it as fact.

Yet again, Buono married another woman shortly after his latest divorce. Deborah Taylor became his bride, but she wouldn't move in with her new husband, which gave him even more freedom to do as he pleased. This included sexually assaulting other women and having a relationship with a teenager who he got pregnant a number of times.

Buono's Partner in Crime is Born

Buono's cousin, Kenneth Bianchi, was also born in New York, almost two decades after his elder relative. His mother was a teenage sex worker with an alcohol problem and, unable to provide her child with the life he needed, she immediately gave him up for adoption upon his birth. The Bianchi's were able to offer the child the security and stability he needed, although this didn't do anything to quell the youngster's penchant for relentless lying from an early age. He also developed something of a terrifying temper and was prone to outbursts of rage when things didn't go his way and was subsequently diagnosed as having a passive-aggressive personality disorder as a child.

ELIZA TOSKA

When Bianchi was six, in 1957, he had a nasty fall from a jungle gym and landed square on his head. After the upsetting event, his mother took him to the doctor as his eyes kept rolling to the back of his head. Bianchi was taken to the doctors frequently by his mother, as he was a frequent bedwetter, and it was noted on the child's medical records that his mother "needed help" with the difficult young boy. By the age of nine, Bianchi was wetting himself so frequently he had to wear sanitary towels. By age 11, he had to move schools due to his inability to get along with his teachers, who thought he wasn't being challenged enough during his studies. His mother disagreed; she thought he was merely angry and inattentive. The following year, he acted out something he'd wanted to do for a while - pulling down a girl's pants. He chose a six-year-old to carry out his cruel fantasy on.

In 1964, his father died, and Bianchi was notably devoid of any emotion. The teen didn't cry or even feign any upset that the man who'd taken care of him for 13 years was dead. As the boy grew older, he began dating and was popular with girls his age. From fifteen through to nineteen, Bianchi showed the makings of a fine young man. He was attentive to his dates, joined a motorcycle club and was courteous to his elders. After he graduated in 1971, he quickly married Brenda Beck, his high school girlfriend, but the marriage only lasted all of eight months.

After this, he enrolled at Monroe Community College with the goal to join the police force but only managed to complete one term. After this, he sought out a job and applied at the sheriff's department but didn't get the role. With few qualifications, he took on odd jobs, one being a security guard at a jewellery store, although it wasn't long before he was caught stealing and fired. The jewellery he stole invariably went to one of his many girlfriends as a gift. His kleptomania stayed with him as he made his way through a number of odd jobs.

Seeking pastures new in 1975, Bianchi moved to LA to live with his cousin, Angelo Buono. Bianchi was enamoured with the lure of Hollywood, the attractive women, the hazy sun-filled days and the endless possibilities that California offered him. He felt like he'd landed on his feet when his cousin showed him the ropes, especially practical things like how to utilise a fake police badge to coerce sex workers into having sex with them for free.

The criminal pair also dreamed up a plan to conjure up some extra cash - they'd become pimps. For a while, they employed Sabra Hannan and Becky Spears to work for them. Bianchi and Buono were terribly violent to the young girls, and as well as pimping them out, they'd beat them, rape them, and keep them locked in their rooms. Luckily, the two women managed to escape before they suffered the same fate as so many would at the hands of the killer cousins.

After this, Bianchi moved in with Kelli Boyd, and in May of 1977, she discovered she was pregnant with his child. He proposed, she rejected him but still maintained a romantic relationship with the father of her child. With their pimping venture on hold due to the girls running away, Bianchi and Buono took action to rebuild their business. They paid Deborah Noble, a sex worker they knew, for what they called a "trick list", which named regular customers who lived in LA. Deborah turned up at Buono's house with her friend, Yolanda

Washington, who was also a sex worker. The pair didn't intend to offer up such personal information to the two cousins and sold them a fake list of names. Despite initially paying for the service, it didn't take Bianchi and Buono long to realise the list they'd bought was phoney. They wouldn't let themselves be swindled by women; they wanted vengeance.

They knew exactly where Yolanda frequented, and in October 1977, they abducted her. They bound her by the legs, wrist and neck and took turns to violently rape her. After they'd strangled her to death, they washed the body and dumped the naked 19-year-old on a hillside close to the Ventura Freeway. Ronald LeMieux, a store owner, would later testify that he saw policemen in an unmarked car flashing their police badges to Yolanda and pushing her into the back seat of their vehicle. This fake badge flashing and leaving the brutalised corpses on the Californians hillsides would become their infamous modus operandi in their slew of sickening murders.

Not even a fortnight later, the Hillside Strangler(s) struck again. They stalked, abducted, raped, and killed a 15-year-old runaway. The young girl had been surviving by selling herself for cash while living on the streets. The evil duo raped the young girl in every way imaginable, sodomising her before dumping her body in a residential area of La Crescenta.

Less than a week later, on November 6, 1977, Elissa Kastin's naked body was found lying in Glendale. She'd been bound at the neck, wrists and ankles, and had been raped and beaten just like the young runaway before her. The sick duo followed Elissa while she drove home from work, pulling her over as she parked up near her home, pretending to be police officers, complete with their usual fake badges and fake police spiel. The young woman knew she'd done nothing wrong, but as she believed the men really were police, she complied with their demands that she get in the back of their car to be taken for questioning.

Around the same time as Elissa's murder, the cousins planned to abduct Catharine Lorre Baker, the daughter of famous actor Peter Lorre. However, the pair were stunned when they found a picture of her and her father among her belongings, and her parentage ensured the killers changed their minds about slaughtering her. After all, they were big fans of Lorre's movie, 'M', where he played a serial killer of children. They set the 24-year-old free, avoiding the attention the murder of a celebrity's child would bring.

By mid-November 1977, 12-year-old Dolores Ann Cepeda and her friend, 14-year-old Sonja Marie Johnson, hopped on a bus to make their way home. When they got off at their stop, a sedan with two men inside rolled up beside them. This was the last time they were seen alive. A few days later, their abused corpses were found by a nine-year-old boy who was playing in a trash heap on the hillside they were dumped on. Both children had been raped, beaten, and strangled to death.

The same day the girls' bodies were discovered, on November 20, 1977, another body turned up. Walkers stumbled upon the lifeless body of Kristina Weckler, who was bloodied and beaten. She had ligature injuries on her ankles, neck and wrists, as well as injuries to her breasts and rectum. An autopsy of the twenty-year-old revealed she'd been injected with glass cleaner.

Three days later, on November 23, another brutalised body turned up near the Golden State Freeway. The woman was identified as Evelyn Jane King, but the severity of her body's decomposition meant it was near impossible to determine if she'd had been raped and beaten like all the other girls who'd turned up dead on the hillsides. Still, the forensics team were able to ascertain she'd been strangled to death. After this particular killing, police decided they needed to do something. They assembled a dedicated task force including officers from the LAPD, the Sheriff's Department and the Glendale Police Department with the intention of bringing the Hillside Strangler to justice.

Around a week later, police found another young woman's body in the Mount Washington hills. Again, the victim had ligature marks on her extremities, as well as visible signs of torture. She had nasty burn marks on her naked body, suggesting the pair had used fire as their weapon of choice this time. The body was identified as Lauren Rae Wagner, and her abduction was witnessed. The woman who saw The Stranglers take Lauren stated two men bundled her into the back of their car. She also offered a description of the possible culprits: one was taller and seemed young - Bianchi - and the other was quite a bit older with unkempt hair - Buono. She'd heard the young woman scream, "You won't get away with this!" as the pair forced her into their vehicle. What the police had been hunting for - "The Hillside Strangler" - was now almost confirmed as two stranglers.

By mid-December, sex worker Kimberly Diane Martin's naked body was found dumped near LA City Hall. As usual, the victim had been tortured and raped. In an attempt to put her own safety first, she joined an escort agency to secure her from the evil clutches of the strangers on the loose. It just so happened that the wicked cousins called her agency to procure their latest victim, and it was Kimberly who was sent out to meet with the client, The Hillside Stranglers.

The address she'd been dispatched to turned out to be an abandoned property that the killers had clearly broken into. The police traced the call from the "client" and found it was made from a Hollywood library.

A helicopter pilot alerted police the following February when he saw an orange Datsun stuck midway on a cliff on the Angeles Crest Highway. When police arrived, they found the naked body of the car's owner stuffed in the trunk of her vehicle. The body had been tortured, showed all of the usual ligature marks the Stranglers were prone to inflicting upon their victims, and she had been raped. She was identified as Cindy Lee Hudspeth, a young student who the killers strangled to death before pushing her car - with her body in - off the cliff.

Her horrific murder, unlike the rest of the Hillside slayings, was unplanned. Cindy had been at Buono's shop discussing the prices of his upholstery service for her car. Bianchi arrived and, as soon as he saw Cindy, took Buono to one side and talked about making the unsuspecting woman their latest victim. It didn't take much to convince Buono that the twenty-year-old deserved to be tortured, raped, and killed.

That same month, The Hillside Stranglers suddenly stopped their reign of terror. The killings ceased. Police were baffled. Around this time, Bianchi had left LA to follow the mother of his child to Washington. She'd rejected his offer of marriage, but Bianchi couldn't let her go. Despite a seemingly fresh start for the young serial killer, it seems his lust for blood followed him wherever he went. Almost a year after the last Hillside Strangler victim, in January 1979, Kenneth Bianchi kidnapped and killed two young women. However, he was never the brains of the operation and without his older cousin there to help clean up the mess, Bianchi did a sloppy job of covering his murderous tracks. The day after the double-murder, police arrested him.

Bianchi had slain the women in the exact same way the Hillside Strangler did, and the murders stopped around the same time he'd departed from LA. Police were certain they'd got the Strangler - one of them at least.

They managed to break the young killer pretty easily. As soon as they mentioned the death sentence, he readily gave up all the details the police wanted, including the name of his accomplice. Buono was also swiftly arrested. Throughout his trial, Bianchi pleaded insanity and insisted he had multiple personalities. The court saw through his self-serving lies. Angelo Buono denied any wrongdoing and stood firm that he was innocent of the ten counts of murder he was being charged with.

In the end, Bianchi changed his plea to guilty for the Washington murders - of which there could be no denial - and just five of The Hillside Strangler slayings. To swerve the death penalty, he testified against the man he once idolised. As a result, he was handed six life sentences and his cousin Buono got life behind bars without the possibility of parole. The jury decided against the use of capital punishment in this case, although the judge stated that, if there was a case where the death penalty was the most appropriate form of justice, this was the case.

Buono died in 2002, while Bianchi is still serving his time behind bars. He made a request for parole in 2010, but this was denied. For crimes like this, it's hard to imagine the killers finding the ability to ever grasp the severity of the wicked things they've done. As of writing this, in mid-2021, Kenneth Bianchi is 70 years old, having spent four decades in jail to think about his crimes. I wonder, if throughout those years, he's felt any remorse for the things he's done, for the young lives he ruthlessly snuffed out and the degradation he and his cousin put their victims through. I suspect both he and his relative would be incapable of such an evolved emotion.

The Sinister Photographer

Things were looking good career-wise for actress Linda Sobek. She'd recently landed a part on the long-running sitcom *"Married With Children"* and was sure this would be the role that would give her acting career the boost she was waiting for. While acting was her passion and the career she wanted to pursue, like all of us, she needed to pay the bills, and that's just what her modelling jobs did. As soon as she graduated from college, while she was a cheerleader for the Los Angeles Raiders, she stepped into the world of modelling. She was pretty, but she wasn't tall - she just grazed five feet four inches - so while fashion modelling was out of the question, her curvy physique and sultry features earned her a number of jobs for swimwear shoots, beer promos, and numerous car magazine shoots.

On the cool Californian morning of November 16, 1995, Linda was heading to a photoshoot, calling her mother as she rushed to the job she was running late for. She was close to her mother, Elaine, and despite risking being late for her upcoming shoot, she still made the time to ring her and go over arrangements for the BBQ her mother was hosting that weekend. Their closeness was well-known, and rarely did a day go by when the pair didn't talk. In fact, it was common for the pair to talk multiple times in a day, so when Linda didn't give her mother a ring later that evening to tell her about her shoot, she knew something was amiss. She worried the entire night, eventually calling Linda's close friend and fellow cheerleader, Brooke Morales, who could perhaps put her mind at ease. By this time, it was the following day, and Brooke didn't have the comforting news Elaine was hoping for. Linda's friend informed the worried mother that the model hadn't shown up for a number of commitments she had that day, including one appointment she wouldn't miss for the world: her wardrobe fitting for her upcoming role in Married With Children. After discussing their worries with one another, Brooke decided to call the police.

Linda lived in Hermosa Beach with her roommates, and this is the first place police looked for her. A subsequent search of the property and questioning of the three people living with her bore no fruit, and police had another blockade in their way: Linda had told no one, not even her mother, where her photoshoot was located the day she vanished.

After two more days passed without so much as a clue, Brooke and Linda's other friends got in touch with TV stations and local newspapers to garner up as much help as possible in spreading the news of Linda's disappearance. As they were doing this, there was finally a break in the case.

That Saturday, a road worker found some items he found interesting in a bin as he worked near Angeles National Forest. He uncovered a stockpile of photos of Linda, a random dairy and the crumpled up receipt for the short-term loan of a Lexus. He carried the photos home, thinking they were nothing sinister until he was watching the news the next day and recognised the girl on his TV was the same as the woman in the picture he collected. Immediately, he called the police, who went straight to the bin where the pictures were found. Sure enough, they found the diary and car rental receipt among the rubbish. They now had their first clue: on the paper rental receipt was a name - Charles Rathbun.

38-year-old Rathbun was a well-known freelance photographer whose work was considered to be top-notch by the numerous Hollywood businesses who hired him. In an unusual twist, police had already been made aware of the name Charles Rathbun in regards to the disappearance of Linda - from Rathbun himself.

He'd contacted police as soon as Linda's disappearance made the news, explaining to them that he'd met with Linda the same day she vanished at a Denny's, where they had an informal meeting about her portfolio and how she could improve her modelling photos. Rathbun advised police that the pair had appointments after their chat, and that was the last he saw of her. Police headed to the Denny's Rathbun told them he met Linda at and they saw her car parked up. There was no sign of Linda, though.

Despite his contacting them with information, police were suspicious of Rathbun. The Lexus receipt bearing his name meant they needed to speak with him, and police prepared to question Charles Rathbun on November 22, but they were called to his home before the intended questioning. When they arrived at his home, they discovered Rathbun drunk, and he was making threats to end his life. He had a female friend with him who'd sustained injuries from him just before police got on the scene. He was subsequently arrested, and through his sobs, he told police he'd killed Linda, although his explanation of what happened is perhaps more shocking than his admission of guilt.

He explained to police that he was taking pictures of Linda for an upcoming promo for the new Lexus. The shoot was located in the Mojave Desert, and between taking shots, Rathbun said he was teaching the aspiring actress to do doughnuts in the car. While exhibiting how to do the high-speed 360-degree turns (intended to cause dust and smoke emit from the car as it's driven in circles) Linda was allegedly stood close by watching him. It was then Rathbun got too close to her with the car and hit her with such force she died. Panicked and at a loss as to what to do next, he drove aimlessly until he decided on a plan of action. In the end, he buried her in the dirt at Angeles National Forest.

Just before police were due to escort Rathbun to show them the body, he made a superficial attempt at killing himself using a disposable razor to cut his wrists. While police didn't truly believe he'd made a serious attempt on his life, and no one but Rathbun knew his true intentions for taking a dull blade to his skin, it's clear he didn't want to lead authorities to where the dead woman lay. Still, within a couple of hours of getting treatment, Rathbun was judged to be in a well enough state to take police to the body. At first, he found it hard to pinpoint where he buried Linda, although this may just have been a futile attempt to prevent the woman's body from being dug up. Regardless, her makeshift grave was found, and she was exhumed from the pit that Rathbun left her in to rot. Immediately it was clear that the decomposing body had no clear signs of being struck at speed by a car - there was no bruising and no wound from the apparent collision.

An autopsy was the next step, during which it was confirmed that Linda hadn't suffered any horrific injuries or broken bones, which would most certainly have been the case if she'd been run over. Plus, there was no blood on the car that apparently struck her, nor was the car dented where Rathbun said he'd hit her. Her blood-alcohol levels showed she had been drinking and could have been drunk, but this can't be confirmed as truth. Since she wasn't kept cool after her murder and was left buried in the desert, the fermentation that then takes place within the body can skew blood-alcohol tests and make them inaccurate.

Despite the uncertainty surrounding her level of drunkenness before her death, there was no doubt about the fact she was sexually assaulted before her murder. The coroner also confirmed what police already strongly suspected: Linda hadn't been hit by a car, but rather she'd been strangled to death. There was blood spatter on the back seat of the Lexus where there was likely a violent struggle between the pair and possibly where she was raped by Rathbun.

There was little room for any doubt at this point: Charles Rathbun sexually assaulted then brutally murdered Linda Sobek with his bare hands. Further background checks on the photographer also raised a number of red flags. In 1979 he was charged with rape in Ohio, his victim a woman who worked with him. She told police that her attacker forced himself upon her, threatening to kill her if she dared to make a noise as he carried out the rape. Afterwards, apparently, Rathbun was apologetic and mentioned he deserved punishment for what he did. However, those words proved to be empty. In the next breath, he told her no one would believe her if she went to the police. His lawyer insisted to the court that the pair engaged in consensual sex and they agreed, acquitting him of the rape.

After this, he seemed to fly under the radar. He moved to LA in 1989, where he turned his knack for photography into a successful freelance business. He specialised in calendar and car shoots. Despite his talent, by some accounts, he was known as being hot-tempered and would get mad when things went wrong and didn't have the ability to admit to his own downfalls or mistakes. As well as his mean-streak, he was also known for being pushy with the models he was shooting - he would come onto them and wouldn't take no for an answer. Some models would refuse to work with him again after some upsetting shoots with him.

After being charged with Linda's murder, Rathbun's already ridiculous story kept changing. His new version of events was that he'd bet the model that she couldn't down a bottle of tequila, which got the small woman drunk. Apparently, she then came onto him. Afterwards, she fell over and hit her head. This, according to Rathbun, explains the dots of blood in the back of the car, and due to her drunkenness, Linda began getting aggressive while sitting in the back seat. Rathbun said he then pinned her down on the seat to calm her down, and after 30 seconds, she stopped fighting back. He said he presumed she was faking it to get him off her. When he did get off her, she wasn't breathing. He placed her limp body on the dry desert and tried to bring her back to life. After this failed, he tied her ankles together and lifted her into the car.

This story was dismissed by the prosecution. They insisted that the photographer didn't even have a job with Lexus requiring him to hire Linda and that he planned the fake shoot in order to either rape her or at the very least come on to her. When he discovered she had no interest in him that way, he turned violent. They told the jury how Charles Rathbun tied Linda up by her ankles and raped her. It was confirmed she'd been sodomised, quite possibly with his pistol. Linda had fought immensely for her life, so much so that the ties that bound her ankles had turned her skin raw. Her final moments were described as Rathbun sitting on her back as her throat was held against an object, with the purpose of suffocating her to death.

Tiffany Richardson, a model who'd previously worked with Rathbun, testified about her time working with the photographer for a 1994 car magazine job. She would go on to expose his deep disdain for the woman he'd murdered, something he'd clearly been feeling for some time: Linda was mentioned during a casual conversation, and Rathbun reportedly spat that she was a "bitch" because she was considered a difficult model to work with. Another model, Amy Weber, also testified about Rathbun's vile remarks about Linda. She told the court how when she worked with him, the pair began batting around potential models' names he could use for a forthcoming magazine shoot he was booked for. Amy mentioned Linda's name as a possible candidate, and she recalled how Rathbun reacted unnecessarily violently, insisting he'd never work with Linda as she was "a little bitch" and ominously stated she would "deserve what she had coming to her." Even at the time, that was an incredibly sinister comment, but in hindsight, it's all the more bodeful.

The trial was followed closely by the press and ended on November 1, 1996, when Rathbun was eventually convicted of the first-degree murder of Linda Sobek. Two days later, he was sentenced to life behind bars without the chance of parole. He was sent to the California Institution for Men, where he remains to this day.

While investigating the killer, police stumbled upon two cold cases that they considered Rathbun the culprit in.

In the spring of 1993, the parts of the skeleton of model Kimberly Pandelios were found lying in the Angeles National Forest. The 20-year-old had gone missing in 1992 after heading out to a modelling gig. The similarities of the Linda Sobek case were eerie, but Rathbun was cleared of any involvement when David Rademaker was sent to jail for the young woman's murder.

Again in 1993, another young girl, Rose Larner, vanished. Following his arrest, Rathbun was the prime suspect for her disappearance due to her living close by the address he had on his driver's licence. Again, he was cleared of this in late 1995 when the 18-year-old's boyfriend was convicted of strangling her to subdue her, slitting her throat to kill her, cutting up her dead body and then setting her remains on fire.

***

MURDERS IN HOLLYWOOD: TRUE CRIME STORIES OF HOMICIDE IN THE HILLS

Thank you for reading *Murders in Hollywood: True Crime Stories of Homicide in the Hills.* In writing this book, I've merged two of my main interests: Hollywood and true crime. The underbelly of LA and the darker side of Tinseltown have always fascinated me, and the lack of books on this frustrated me, so I wrote one of my own! I truly hope you enjoyed it, and the crimes I've covered have made you think. Even those with seemingly privileged lives and living somewhere as hedonistic as Hollywood aren't immune to the evil that stalks this world.

If you enjoyed this book or would like to see similar books from me, I would be ever so grateful if you'd leave a review. They help so much in getting my work out there. I really appreciate you making it this far, and I can't thank you enough for choosing me for your latest true crime read. Here's to many more!

- Eliza Toska, 2021

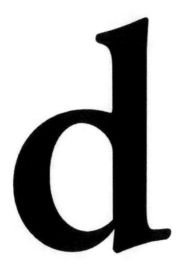

About the Publisher

Dimension Books is a UK based non-fiction publisher specialising in true cime and intriguing real-life events.

Find us at Dimensionbooks.com and on social media.

CPSIA information can be obtained
at www.ICGtesting.com
Printed in the USA
BVHW031215030822
643544BV00025B/2066